Wisdom Can Speak At An Early Age

Mattie Wilson

Inspired by Everyday Life Experiences

To order additional copies of this book, contact:
Xlibris
844-714-8691
www.Xlibris.com
Orders@Xlibris.com

ISBN: Softcover   978-1-4415-7064-2
        EBook   978-1-6641-2027-3

Print information available on the last page

Rev. date: 05/22/2021

Photography by: Mattie Wilson & Gloria Crockett

To my mother Gloria, and grandmother Ethel, who both raised me with nothing but love; to my two siblings Elsie, and EJ; to my wonderful niece and nephew Devontae and Jasmine. To my two wonderful, joyful, and comical sons Cecil and Isaac, I

love you all with all my heart.

CONTENTS

LIFE

THE

Beating of the heart, when meeting

Exciting old or brand new people, and the

Sunshine across your face, when the

Thunder storms' and Lightning aren't so bad after

all.

Water is the main source of life

And a way to cleanse the soul, which leaves

Yesterday as the past and today there's a chance

TO

Love and be loved, and to remember

I am somebody awesome, that is

Very important in the eye of the Highest, to

Experience the wrong to make it right;

By caring for everyone,

Especially the one's

Who love you the most.

Live your life with a good heart and your struggles will come out golden!

TOMBOY

When I was a kid;
I started noticing things
Going wrong in my home,
My dad was always gone.

When my dad was around
I wanted his attention.
Not only just for me
But for my two siblings.

Then my dad started to take,
My big sis' and I with him.
My sis' knew right away,
I was young-I found out a bit late.

Then he started taking us to the park instead.
We only played games that were for boys
But I made sure I perfected the sport,
So that he wouldn't be shamed.

Later I threw away my Barbie's
Or tried to flush them down the toilet.
Then borrowed my friend's skate board
I played hard like a boy.

I thought my dad would stay
But something must have gone wrong;
Because later we had to move away,
Away to a whole other state.

We moved close to Grandma's house
My mom's mother,
The one grandma that showed
A lot of love.

I didn't know if
I would see my dad again.
So the TOMBOY stayed within,
It helped with the situation I was in.

This was a new town
But there were still bully's around;
In Texas, I helped my friends,
Now I had to fight for my brother.
Also, I had to beat up a boy once,
For trying to touch my goods by force.
You have to be tough-
Living in Monroe Project Hoods.

I learned that the boys and girls
Here were very fast.
I had to be tough
But I was never bad,
I was good and quiet in class.

At home I would climb trees
I loved being me.
I would climb to sit on the roof;
To star gaze,
To look at great magazines,
Or to read romance books.

I would only hang with the boys
That was my friends,
I was happy being one of them.
Didn't have to show them my goods
They respected me,
And I really missed them
When I left the hood.

Live your life with a good heart and your struggles will come out golden!

MOTHER

YOU are truly my **M**other

I wish of no **O**ther

Always helping **T**ill this Day

Praying for me and **H**ealing me

YOU teach me **E**very day

I appreciate your **R**eal love.

MY GRANDMA

Mother of my Mother

Yes she's my Grandma

And an

Great Mother to my two sibs and me.

Really nice and gentle

Always around to help us

Never saying No!

Daring us to always try

Mother of my Mother

Always ready to care

And I'm glad to have her love.

She's the jewel in my box.

And no matter the age,

She's still that sparkle in my life.

Live your life with a good heart and your struggles will come out golden!

SENIOR

You wish it was you,

To get to do the things that we do.

Hold up a sec. you can too;

If you don't clown around,

Or act like a fool.

You will be a **SENIOR** some day

Too bad it couldn't be in "**02**"!

Live your life with a good heart and your struggles will come out golden!

POOR

Sometimes I wished I was born wealthy!
I now thank God I was born just healthy.
But being poor is very hard at times:
The bills pile up when I wished they wouldn't
        No matter how hard I try to save
        I always end up needing what I had put
        away.
Then I find myself looking for other ways . . .
Other ways to get the bills paid:
        Like playing my last five dollars
        Just to play the lottery.
        Or being dropped off at the Bingo Hall;
        Hoping to win BIG,
        To be able to pay next months rent,
        And to be able to end the stress.
Or HURT myself even more by:
        Giving plasma for a check of thirty-five or
        forty-five,
        To put gas in the tank for two weeks;
        Working myself to the point I know I
        shouldn't,
        Or until sickness overwhelms me.

Being a single mother isn't always easy either
But I had these little people
And I plan to keep them.
I want them to feel happy
I want them to feel loved
I struggle for the joy of my boys:
Whether it's to get pampers or diapers
It's hard, but I'm a fighter;
Or high priced medicine
I'll find good ways to get it;
And if they aren't feeling well
I always pay attention,
I'm always there.
I didn't plan on being a Single Mother,
It just happened:
Fell for him, got married, had kids
And he failed our relationship.
He never knew how to love me
And he never wanted to learn either.
So I'm stuck providing
For our two little people on my own.
They know it but don't quite understand yet,
I don't want them to have any worries
I just want them to feel blessed.

Live your life with a good heart and your struggles will come out golden!

MY HANDS, MY FEET

My hands and my feet are wonderful:
But a bit rough;
And you would be too,
If you only knew-
What they have been through.

I wish I would not have,
But they have been through combat.
Now they hurt, pop,
And sometimes crack.
They still work & that I am glad!

I now see the scars,
And I now see the wrinkles.
They work too hard;
Beat up like being behind bars,
Or fighting-battling a real war.

Cream, lotion, or Vaseline,
Nothing works on them.
They have been through a lot,
It will take forever-
To get them back soft.

Live your life with a good heart and your struggles will come out golden!

HARD WORKER

I am truly a hard worker:
If a job is too hard for me
I keep trying
Until I have to listen to my body.
I have to slack off a bit
But I really never quit.
Unless the job puts me in jeopardy
Or until the boss dismisses me;

I might take off some days
But only when I'm sick
And I need to rest.
That does not mean
I get to stay in the house,
I'm a single parent.
I never actually get to rest
Not even when I was married;

Hurt or sick,
I still have to run errands.
There are always things I need to go get,
There's always food I need to fix,
There are always hungry boys I need to feed,
There are always dirty boys I need to bath,
There's always something that needs cleaning
Thank God I now live close to FAMILY!

My brain never sleeps!
Not even when I am a sleep
It has to dream of work.

Chiefly when I'm injured,
I have to endure the pain
Because I am truly a hard worker!

Live your life with a good heart and your struggles will come out golden!

I Missed My Love

I missed you my love

I wished you were here,

You were too far away

I wished you were near.

There was no need to leave

I wished you had stayed.

I needed you with me;

To feel your tender embrace,

To bless me with your grace,

And to love me face to face.

Live your life with a good heart and your struggles will come out golden!

I WANTED YOU!

I wanted you:
> *Outside by the ocean*
> *Yes, on the gritty sand*
> *With you rubbing me with*
> *your hands.*

> *Inside on the carpeted floor*
> *Hard, leaning on the door*
> *All night until the next morn.*

Everyday I wanted too . . .
Since you were my guy
I had to satisfy that desire in your
eyes.
But it was complicated,
I tried to explain myself to you.

"Yes, I wanted you,
Then working hard
Made me blue.
You didn't understand-
What was going on in my brain;
Tiredness, sleep, and body pains."

"Afterward, I only wanted
you . . .
To just hold me
And let me sleep.
Then I would have wanted you
A lot more, more, and more that
day."

Live your life with a good heart and your struggles will come out golden!

SOARING TO SUCCEED

There upon a tree,
A black bird sound a sleep.

So comfortable in her nest,
She pulled her babies close to her chest.

Later, almost in the moon light,
She has to take flight before the sunrise.

Soaring low across the sky,
Looking for away with eyes wide.

She has to get the bait,
Before her babies awake.

Knowing, if she doesn't succeed,
This would be another day-
That her babies she couldn't feed.

SNAKES IN MY LANE

I just heard that there were-
Slithering devils outside my new home.
Coming from the back pit,
Down inside the deep ditch.

They came out
When the canal was full,
From the heavy rain.
So they decided they wanted to graze.

Wandering in another's predators lane
Not knowing what the other opponent would
think
Or to play the game-
To definitely win!

If you craw or even peak through my fence
Don't slide by my little ones!
For the safety of my own,
I will have to defend.

I pray that you stay where you live,
Or I may get seriously offended.
The bible says:
"Thy shalt not kill",
But In due time I will.
I will do anything-
To protect the life of my kids.

Live your life with a good heart and your struggles will come out golden!

STILL LEARNING
STILL CHANGING

I may be an old soul
In a young body.
That is why I know
That I am still learning,
And I am still changing.

I learn by watching.
I learn by listening.
Then I make a change,
Or help make a change;
By caring for myself,
Or caring for someone else.

I know that my body is still changing
I know that my mind is still learning,
I know that nothing stays the same.
And that some changes maybe difficult
And some changes I just can't take,
But it is okay to let that change slip away.
I don't have to hold on to the change
If the change isn't for me.

I admit that I am still learning
And I admit that I am still changing.
Now I accept what I can't change;
And move on for my kids and myself,
And wait for what tomorrow may bring.

Live your life with a good heart and your struggles will come out golden!

Love Is In The Heart!

If everybody would just love everybody
As you love yourself,
No one would be capable
    of hurting others on purpose.

In general, they hate themselves;
That is why they treat people ugly.

That is why it is hard to forgive,
When u know that person will do it again.

Actions do speak way louder than words;
In addition, words do not mean a thing,
If they are not coming from where
    the love starts-in the heart.

Love does not come from the brain.
Most people think from the brain
    and not from the heart.

If your heart is not in it;
To stay faithful,
Then your brain will fail you.

You cannot learn love alone;
You have to know it deep in your heart
You would not hurt the person you love.

If you do not know it in your heart
Then you do not know anything.
You are just a fool
With no wisdom at all!

Live your life with a good heart and your struggles will come out golden!

STRESS COMES FROM?

Taking money from the hard earn income

Adding more cents to your dollar

EXcelling at making life a lot harder, to

Empty out the Earth, making

Society more unhealthy due to stress,

To keep us with more bills-medically,

and to help the baby booming world disappear.

Live your life with a good heart and your struggles will come out golden!

STRESSED OUT!

I want to be left alone
To myself at my own home,
They do not know what I am about
Sometimes I do not know myself,
Because I am just stressed out.

Kind of tired of them uneducated haters
However, I have to love my neighbors,
Feeling sad and kind of mad
I just need to shout,
I need to lie down
So I won't be too stressed out.

Never say, "You can not wait till you're grown"
Live every minute right until you're gone,
Love more and you'll never be alone.
But Players keep singing the same song,
They avoid that cheating is plain wrong.

This is why I will hide from the world now
Trying not to worry about the next route.
Where would I be in 4 years?
I don't know now
Because I'm all stressed out.

Trying to take in life day by day
And thanking God my soul didn't break,
Happy for every breath I take.
Learning through the unwanted changes
Do you understand what I'm saying?
I don't know myself
I'm way pass stressed out!

Live your life with a good heart and your struggles will come out golden!

JESUS

He the son of God,

Who is not dead

He watches

over thy head.

From morning

till night,

You hit the bed and wake up all right.

For a chance to start life, brand new.

He is still alive . . .

He lives in me

and He lives in you.

Just try to do

what He would do

And bring a

change

for the GOOD!

Live your life with a good heart and your struggles will come out golden!

FOR LIFE ISN'T DESTINED

My soul speaks of sorrow,

Because my soul is restless.

The way that life is rolling

There might not be a tomorrow.

Love is not about the money;

But people marry only to not feel lonely,

Never to stay for ever,

Only to stray where ever.

There's no reason to look.

Why go look for the wrong,

When the right is in front of you.

And only God has the answers.

So I'm going to remember that

The next day maybe forbidden.

I'm going to listen when destiny whispers;

There are no promises to awaken,

Therefore, everyday is a blessing.

Live your life with a good heart and your struggles will come out golden!

MANY STRIDES OF STRUGGLES

There's only one world
That appears to be in the light.
When the unthinkable is done
In the shadows of darkness.
One world where they wonder
What's under the covers?
Never to look for the answers on top.

Being in this one world
Destruction is only promised.
Generations after generations
The world will only get worse.
There's no safe way to save this Earth,
The pain won't stop,
And the hurt won't go away!

In this one world
That man rules this earth;
Love won't combine with joy,
Love will be combined with death,
So peace will never be in the Middle East.

Until that journey to the pearly gates
All one can do is pray,
And leave the darkness behind.
Never look at the pass
Not even one single glance,
It is the only way to shut out the bad.

Ride your struggles till you get
To the steps of the THRONE.
Walk your many strides
With your head held high.
Let faith guide your struggle into the right,
You need to be the one
To have the gift of everlasting life.

Live your life with a good heart and your struggles will come out golden!

SECRETS LIES BENEATH

Who can tell what is in a gray sky,

Or the problems behind clouded eyes,

Or why their winds howl at night.

Black shadows in the dark;

Not to bring neither happiness nor joy,

But to bring despair to the heart.

They start to mistake alleys for dead ends,

Blowing against the walls to no where

Dwelling there—seeking to begin.

Trying to start brand new from the torn life.

But the winds never die,

It moves in a warm breeze on to other lives.

CLASSLESS WOMEN

You dirty classless women,
Always wanting another woman's man
Never wanting to work hard to get your own,
Tearing apart a hard working woman's home.

You don't know anything about respect,
So why should you be treated with it.
You open your legs-
To anyone who could care less.
You think you're beautiful by the way;
You do your hair or the way you dress,
Girl that fakeness is a mess.

He will always live in regret,
And wished that you and he never met.
When I leave him he's going to be with someone else,
And you, you will only be by your damn foolish self.
You was only worth your sex,
Which you could have kept.

But men are never satisfied.
So they put lust and adultery to the test;
And the classless women think that they won,
Because his real woman left.
But you aren't worth a penny!
My man will soon leave you alone;
He's missing me-now that I'm gone,
Now you're by yourself-again with no man,
Wishing you had one!

Live your life with a good heart and your struggles will come out golden!

I WONDER . . .

If I was thinner, would you still be with me;

If I was a lot finer, would you still run off to cheat?

If I would have lost all the baby weight, would your eyes still stray;

If I was a better wife, would you still take HER out on that date?

If I wasn't so bossy, would you still stay out late;

If I would have satisfied you more, would you still take that drank?

If I didn't fuss and fight, would you have helped clean the house?

AND

I WONDER . . .

If you weren't as bossy as well, would we still have argued;

If you wouldn't have had to go OVER THERE,

would you still act a fool?

If you would have showed me your real ego,

would I still have our two little people?

If you didn't drink, would we have been together today;

If you hadn't neglected me, would I have stayed?

Now I don't wonder anymore,

Because the marriage is too far apart-

And it maybe too far over.

Live your life with a good heart and your struggles will come out golden!

JUST WALK ON BY

You say you want to know why I'm crying
Well, look into my eyes
And not at my body
Would you recognize?
The reason why?
No, because you're not
Looking at the pain in my face
I can see that
You're too busy thinking
What's under my shirt,
In my pants, between my legs?
You think I need sex
When all I need is a friend.

Can you be that friend?
To over come sin
And listen from within?
By the way you're looking
I don't think you can.
You talk and you conversed
About how your God is great.
Knowing your lustful ways
Only came to take.

You think you're helping me,
When your attempts mean to misuse.
And now like I sensed,
You feel up against my goods.
When I refused—
You apologize, "say you didn't mean to."
But now when I call to talk,
You give a lame excuse.
Leaving me more confused.
You didn't want a friend
You only wanted me to do you.

Now you add to the pain
You failed to help in the first place.
So . . .
Next time you see
A pretty lady crying,
Just walk on by
If you only intend on lying.

Live your life with a good heart and your struggles will come out golden!

I'M JUST LOOKING . . .

To feel the wind blow under the moon,
For the leaves to fall in the Fall.

For the feel of sunshine on my face,
To feel the warmth from the sun in the Winter.

For the flowers to grow and the colors to show,
To see the beauty of the season Spring.

To feel the cool breeze underneath the Magnolia Tree,
For the feel of ice-cold lemonade in the Summer.

I'm just looking for a place to breath,
For a place to feel free.

I'm not looking for a place to feel guilty,
You have to understand why I'm just looking.

I'm looking for some one to be my best bud,
And for someone whose mind is beautiful and fun.

I'm looking for love, but not all of yours;
See I only have half a heart,
So I can only promise a little part.

Half was torn from all the lies,
The other half barely survived.

So don't get mad and beg me please,
Or stop talking to me.

When life gets too complicated,
All I'm looking for is a good Christian friend.

Live your life with a good heart and your struggles will come out golden!

Memories

I was cleaning out my house one day
Trying to throw away a lot of clutter.
I thought it was mostly trash.
Then I noticed my Journal,
It held old memories from the past.
It automatically opened to a page,
Book marked; *"Wedding Plans,
Songs to Burn to CD"*,
The songs were mostly by *Marques Houston,
Dru, Hill* and *Jodeci*.
I was probably going to write more songs,
As the days went on.
However, there was nothing else,
I had stopped right there.

I started remembering we never
Had a real wedding,
And I was waiting for the day
To invite all our family.
All we had was a ceremony,
With just us saying I do.

But it is ironic!
That today was our 5th Anniversary,
Yet it is almost over.

Though, we are separated,
I am technically still his wife-
Until he sends the papers to sign.

He did not call me
and I was not about to call him either.

After I trashed plenty of junk,
I went through some more stuff.
Then I got distracted by some old pictures.
I started to go trough them,
Then I closed the book quickly.
I started to feel the sickness:
Then I started to feel the tears,
One finally escaped running down-
my cheeks passed my ears.
It is hard remembering the rocky-
4 (that would have been 5) years.

I had made up my mind;
I did not want to remember any more,
So I sat the trash out side and closed the door.
I would definitely throw it out in the morning,
Every part of me wished-
this was already over.
But deep inside-

Live your life with a good heart and your struggles will come out golden!

something wants to hold on.
That is when I realized,
I am still in love with him.

So I told myself "NO!
It maybe time to love someone else,
Some one that really cares.
No more lonely nights waiting alone;
Some one else is happy-
to fill that whole in your home,
Some one else that truly wants you everyday-
and every night in his arms."

"Some day some one else
will want you as part of his rib!
You can make new memories-
with someone who has real feelings,
And you can forget the misery."

Though it is a sin to remarry:
One special day;
"You will walk down that aisle-
a second time,
Hand and hand-you and he will repent,
You know God will not leave you lonely,
He will forgive both of your sins."

Live your life with a good heart and your struggles will come out golden!

To Fall or Not To Fall

Sometimes war is good
And most times war is bad
Some times fighting the right battle
helps you win freedom
But when the right fights aren't won
War can be evil!

"So to every alive or fallen soldier
Your bravery will never be forgotten,
And your soul will be remembered."

"You fought hard and you fought long
You even had to leave your loved ones,
To travel far away from home."

Some went for good
And some went for the money,
Little did they know what was coming?

Some had lost their lives:
With a loud whistle;
It has no name when it hits,
Boom! The explosion comes quick!

Some lost their limbs:
Now are desperately trying to adjust;
Without any luck
Hoping to get over the depression,
To stop misusing the alcohol,
And to stop misusing the medication.

Some lost their minds:
They don't know which way to go
Or who to trust,
Still fighting when everything is alright.

Some lost their spirit:
The joy nor the laughter isn't in them
They can't enjoy life any more,
Every turn seems wrong down the long road.

Some lost their families;
Or the people they once loved.
The neglect, the hurt, and the pain . . .
Soon everyone strays away.

We failed at one thing:
Saving ourselves from being the slave;
Therefore WAR only makes life worse,
Jesus is our only SAVIOR,
All we can do is pray.

Live your life with a good heart and your struggles will come out golden!

THE BEAUTY

The beauty of art is all around!
On the smooth grooves of wood,
In the volume of a lions roar,
In the mold of the mountains that stand high-
reaching toward the sky,
And in every fluff of a cloud.

Beauty is every where:
Within the volume of a person's voice,
A beat that makes a certain noise,
Or the reason we make music for.

All around in the shape of a human being,
In the color or the length of a person's hair,
In the clothes that they wear.
Deep down in their soul,
Beauty lies where no one knows.

Art, where volume is a must
And texture is a thickness that beauty comes from.
There's a variety of lights and dark;
But what will come of beauty?
If everyone lives are cut short,
One without the other, life couldn't start.

There would be no sign of life;
No wonder's of giving birth,
No singing "JOY" at church.
There wouldn't be a place called Earth.

I advise you to pay attention to the leaves
that falls from the trees,
Because we are in a rage
that is killing society;
We always start all kinds of war,
We fight and cause destruction,
Leaving beauty to bleed,
And leaving someone in need.

Look in front of your eyes
Beauty is what we need to keep!

Live your life with a good heart and your struggles will come out golden!

THE STORM

It looks too bad to bring out the grill
And maybe too late
When the storm ends:

Now the thunder starts roaring loud.
Then I see lightning through
Each gray cloud,
Brightening the dull gray sky.

Then the danger struck the power lines,
There was no light around for miles,
Not even from the stars up high.

The rain filled the-
Oceans and lakes nation wide.
Not even the boats near the coast
Could survive.

I hear the aggressive wind and rain
Beating down my window pane,
As I strained to hear myself think.

Next the lightning touched down
From the sky, bright as day light,
Then suddenly it was blacker than night.

It's too loud and too violent
It sounds really near.
Don't listen to the sound
Cover thy ears.

Such evil, no one should fear,
Try not to be afraid
To open your eyes to see,
That the storm has cleared.

Live your life with a good heart and your struggles will come out golden!

Printed in the United States
by Baker & Taylor Publisher Services